The Unsticker

Peter Freeth

CGW
PUBLISHING

2017

The Unsticker

Peter Freeth

Third Edition: October 2017

ISBN 978-1-908239-32-9

© Peter Freeth 2000 - 2017

Published by: www.cgwpublishing.com

CGW Publishing   mail@cgwpublishing.com
B 1502
PO Box 15113   **www.theunsticker.com**
Birmingham
B2 2NJ   www.nenlp.com
United Kingdom   www.geniuslearning.co.uk

Visit www.theunsticker.com to learn more about how this amazing problem solving tool works, and also to find the free online and smartphone versions.

The Unsticker is an amazing problem solving tool that uses the power of the right questions to unravel even the stickiest of problems.

Many people have said that, after only 4 or 5 questions, they can't even remember what their problem had been! The Unsticker will, at the very least, change the way you thought about a problem, making it much easier to tackle.

To use The Unsticker, simply take a moment to think of the problem that you want to solve, then follow these four simple rules:

Select questions randomly
If you turn to random pages, you'll tend to use only the middle of the book. Look around you for numbers, use digits from telephone numbers, roll dice, throw darts, use a random number generator, ask a stranger to pick a number.

Ask every question that you select
Don't look for a 'good question', and don't skip any questions if they don't make sense. The Unsticker works *because* the questions don't, at first, make sense.

Take time to properly consider every question
It helps to have someone else ask you the questions so that you can take time to think of your answer. If you're using The Unsticker by yourself, make sure you take time to form a full answer for each question.

Keep asking questions until the problem changes
That's all there is to it!

1

What is it that you don't want to happen?

2

When was the problem past its 'best before' date?

3

Are you secretly in love with this problem?

You and the problem sitting in a tree

4

Imagine your best friend has the problem. What is your advice to them?

5

How many
lightbulbs does
it take to
change the
problem?

6

SO

WHAT?

7

If you painted
the problem
green, would
anyone mistake
it for a big, round
cabbage?

8

Is the problem colourful or grey?

9
WHAT
DO
YOU
WANT
MOST
OF
ALL?

If a fairy godmother granted you three wishes, would solving this problem *really* be one of them?

11

What would happen if you didn't?

12

Is the problem somewhere, everywhere, nowhere or anywhere?

13

What's the unlucky number for the problem?

14

If this problem
were a person,

where would you
hit them?

15

Where would this problem be without you?

16

Who else does this involve?

17

Which breed of
dog would be
best at fetching
this problem if
you threw it
away?

18

If your

PROBLEM

was made into a
movie, who
would play the
problem?

19

How do you
know?

20

How does the problem look in a mirror?

21

If you turned this problem on its head, how would it smell?

22

Do you need anyone else to do this for you?

23
IS THE PROBLEM HALF FULL OR HALF EMPTY?

24
WHAT WOULD HAPPEN IF YOU DEFLATED THE PROBLEM A LITTLE MORE?

25

Is the problem wrinkly or sprinkly?

26

What time is the

problem?

27
What shape is that problem?

28
Does the problem sink or float?

∿∿∿∿∿∿∿∿∿∿∿∿∿∿∿∿∿∿∿∿∿∿

29

How does the
problem look on
fast forward?

30

AFTER YOU'VE SOLVED THE PROBLEM, WHO WILL YOU CELEBRATE WITH?

31

Is the problem pointy or smoothy?

32

If you let the problem do a bungee jump, would you secretly make the rope too long?

33

What will you do?

34

In a TV talent show, how far would the problem get before being buzzed off?

35

When is the problem's sell by date?

How
is the
problem
going?

37

HOW DOES THE PROBLEM LOOK THROUGH THE WRONG END OF A TELESCOPE?

38

What would a child make with this problem?

39

IF YOU PAINTED THE PROBLEM PURPLE, WOULD ANYONE MISTAKE IT FOR AN ENORMOUS JUICY BIG AUBERGINE?

40

What mustn't you do?

41
How slow is this problem?

42
Is the problem warm or cool?

43
Are you an antidisenproblematarian?

44

WOUL
DTHE
PROB
LEM
PASSAN
EYEEXAM

45

What happens if you turn the contrast of the problem up?

46
What happens when you turn the sound down on the problem?

47
When isn't a problem a problem any more?

48
WHICH SUPERHERO WOULD HAVE THIS PROBLEM AS AN ARCH ENEMY?

49
How would a baker roll out the problem?

50

If this problem was a country, what kind of government would it have?

51

When did you first know about this?

52

What would happen if you did?

53

What sizes does your problem come in?

54

Is the problem somewhere over a rainbow?

55

What would it be like to fly the problem like a kite?

56

How much do you enjoy the attention you got from having had this problem?

57

Is the problem

near

or

far?

58
Which part of this problem is the most spiky?

59
If you put this problem in a blender, what colour would the purée be?

60

How does this problem help you?

61

Which letters and numbers have brought you today's problem?

62

If this problem were a shop, what shop would it be?

63

IS THE PROBLEM LIGHTER AT THE TOP OR AT THE BOTTOM?

64

Is the problem
wrapped in
aluminium foil
or cling film?

65

What stops you
from doing what
you have already
decided to do?

66
How would a gangster deal with the problem?

67

If you complained in a restaurant about this problem, what would the waiter say?

68

How would a mouse tackle this problem?

Is the problem here or there?

70

What have you done to **earn** this problem?

71

IF YOU WRAP YOURSELF UP IN A COSY WARM DUVET, HOW DOES THE PROBLEM FEEL?

72

This question has been removed for your safety. Could you try another?

73

What kind of cloud would this problem make?

74
What would you do?

75
If this problem were a fruit, what fruit would it be?

WHAT POTION WOULD A WITCH MAKE WITH THE PROBLEM?

77

If you painted the problem blue, would anyone mistake it for a piece of sky?

78

Has the problem's fuse blown?

79

When you look back on the problem, what will make you **laugh** most?

80

If this problem were a vegetable, what vegetable would it be?

81

When were the ends of the problem easier to find?

82

What would you do if you could?

83

If you could cook with this problem, which part would be inedible?

84

WHAT IF?

85

If you could paint
this problem,
which colour
would you use
third?

86

Is the problem
left or right?

87

If you look at the problem through a microscope, what do you discover?

88

How would a poacher hunt the problem?

89

What happens if you turn the brightness of the problem up too much?

90

IS THE PROBLEM RIPE YET?

91

If you unravelled the problem, how many scarves could you make out of it?

92

What will you do differently next time?

93

Is the problem
seriously worse
than spiders?

94

How does the problem
sound at the wrong
speed?

95

What won't you do?

96

Which political party would put this problem in its manifesto?

97

What does the problem taste like?

98

If you used a periscope to look over the top of the problem, what would you see?

99

How will having had this problem have helped you?

100
Do you want an
apple pie with
your problem?

101
Where would
this problem
hold a tea party?

102

Is the problem

fuzzy or

sizzly?

103

Can you try as
hard as you can
to remember?

104

What's the one thing you would like most of all, right now?

105

What would you do if things weren't the same?

106
What kind of cake could solve this problem?

107
Is the problem tied up with string or ribbon?

108

Why don't you stop playing with your problem? It's not a toy, you know.

109

How far can the problem fall?

110
What shouldn't you do?

111
Is the problem wider at the start or at the end?

112

How has the problem changed tomorrow?

113

When did you first start to think this way?

114

If the problem went to a fancy dress party, what would it dress up as?

115

Who would vote for the problem?

116

How would an incompetent doctor diagnose the problem?

Dr Hackenbush will see you now

117

What does the problem mean?

118

When is was it?

119
IF YOU CLOSE YOUR EYES, HOW DOES THE PROBLEM LOOK?

120
Are you certain this is your problem?

Was this a problem a month ago?

122
How do you actually know that this is a problem for you?

123
When is the problem past its bedtime?

ZZZZZZZZZZZZZZZZ

124

Would you rather look at the problem through the round, square or arched window?

How does the problem look on rewind?

126

Why are you reading this instead of solving your problem?

127

How shiny is this problem?

128

What would make the biggest difference to you, right now?

129

What if this was really someone else's problem?

130

How would the problem be treated by airport baggage handlers?

131

When did you last worry about this?

132

Did you enjoy
the sympathy
that this problem
got for you?

133

If this problem
was a country,
what would its
flag look like?

134
Which stand up comedian could you sell your problem to?

135
When will you have solved this problem yet?

136

How many 'dislikes' would this problem get on Facebook?

137

Was this a problem a week ago?

138

How could you make money out of this problem?

Is the
problem
like a tub
or a lid?

140
Would the problem go off if you didn't keep it in the fridge?

141
Was this a problem a year ago?

142

What the f

CENSORED

king idiot?

143

What would a celebrity chef make with this problem?

144

When did you last think about this?

145

The program problem.exe has crashed. Please try again. If the error persists, consult your user guide for more information.

146
What colour is this problem?

147
As you see yourself with this problem, what strikes you as odd?

148

If you donated this problem to a charity shop, what would they say?

149

Is the problem held together with sticky tape or glue?

150
What kind of animal could solve this problem?

151
Bang! And the problem's gone!

152
What can't you
do?

153
As you see
yourself with
that problem,
what strikes you
as funny?

154

Have you looked for the problem's reset button?

155

How is this problem an **ego boost** for you?

156

Can you think of a time when you knew you were free to want whatever you wanted?

157

How high does the problem float?

158

Imagine it's a week from now. How has the problem changed?

159

How would a carpenter saw the problem?

160

What would archaeologists of the future think if they dug up the problem?

161

What spice would you add to the problem?

162

When do you want this to change?

163

Why don't you?

164
What does the problem sound like?

165
How does the phase of the moon affect this problem?

How light is the problem ?

167

If you had a voodoo doll for this problem, where would you stick the pins?

168

Where are you without the problem?

169
How else can the problem not be more or less?

170
Who cares enough about you to help you?

171

What are you stopping yourself from **doing**?

172

Imagine it's ten years from now. How has the problem changed?

173

Who can you
turn to?

174

What are you

not allowing

yourself to think

about doing?

175

If you stick cotton wool in your ears, how does the problem sound?

176

WHAT SHOULD YOU DO?

177

IMAGINE IT'S A MONTH FROM NOW. HOW HAS THE PROBLEM CHANGED?

178

What wouldn't happen if you did?

179

What if you were wrong about this?

180

If you ran this problem up the flagpole, who would salute?

181

Think of someone you know who you envy. What would they do?

182

Is the problem better boiled, fried or sautéed?

183
Can you?

184
Are you worrying about the *right* problem?

185
Why bother?

186
IMAGINE YOUR FAVOURITE CARTOON CHARACTER HAS THIS PROBLEM. WHAT IS YOUR ADVICE TO THEM?

187
How does this problem smell?

188
Imagine the problem is down in a valley, and you're up on the hill. What feels different?

189

Is there something more important beneath this?

190

Would the problem taste better with a little more or less salt?

191

Does the
problem **boing**
or **bong**?

192

*What would an
antiques dealer
say about the
problem?*

193

What will be the best thing about having had this problem?

194

Are we there yet?

Is the problem

firm or

WOBBLY?

Hot dog.
Corn dog.
What
would a
problem
dog be
like?

197

What happens if you turn the brightness of the problem down?

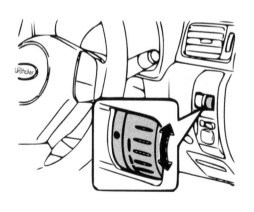

If you stuck a pin
in the problem,
would it go 'pop'
or
'psssssssssssss
ssssssssssssssss
ssssssssssssssss
ssssssssssssssss
ssssssssssssss'

199

If you received a telesales call from this problem while you were eating your dinner, what would you say?

200
How does the problem look through a kaleidoscope?

201
When was the last time you forgot that problem's name?

202

Which part of this problem is the most ticklish?

203

Is the problem held up by braces or a belt?

204

What do you want to happen?

What would happen if you inflated the problem a little **TOO MUCH**?

Why do you want this problem?

207
What rhymes
with the
problem?

208
What are the main
differences
between the
problem and a
picnic?

What would be the
worst question for
me to ask you right
now?

210

What happens

as you walk

further away and

the problem gets

smaller and smaller and smaller?

211

Who can you trust?

212

Does your

problem enjoy

going for a walk?

213

Error: This problem is no longer available. Please refresh your browser.

214

What has this problem got to do with **you**?

215

What must you do?

216

Is the problem really a **symptom** of something else?

217

How far does the problem **stretch?**

218

When did you first find out about this?

219

What does this problem prove?

220
Is the problem up...

...or down?

221

What kind of
fossil will this
problem
become?

222

Can you think
of a single
good reason to
keep this
problem?

223
What makes you important enough to have a problem like this?

224
What would this problem look like on top of a cake?

225

Would you push the problem over a cliff while no-one was looking?

226

How could the problem benefit someone else?

227

Does the problem ring or clang?

228

Imagine your parent has this problem. What is your advice to them?

229

If the problem was made into a movie, who would play the part of you?

230

Would a witch
make the problem
disappear with a
whoosh or a bang?

231

When is it
problem
season?

RABBIT
SEASON

DUCK
SEASON

PROBLEM
SEASON

232

Is someone up there trying to tell you something?

233

If you drop the problem, does it *smash* or **thud**?

234
What would a famous artist make out of the problem?

235
If this problem were a musical instrument, what instrument would it be?

How heavy is the problem?

237
If the problem went on a celebrity fad diet, what would it lose?

238
Is the problem sweet or sour?

239

What kind of car
could run over
this problem?

240

How will
having had
this problem
have changed
you?

241

Which is worse, this problem or running out of milk?

242

If you got home and found that the shop hadn't charged you for this problem, would you own up?

243

As you see yourself with this problem, what strikes you as curious?

244

Is the problem available in other colours?

245

Which platform
does the problem
leave from?

246

Did you
secretly enjoy
having this
problem?

If you painted
the problem
orange, who
would mistake
it for a
pumpkin?

How much will

you **miss**

having

this

problem

around?

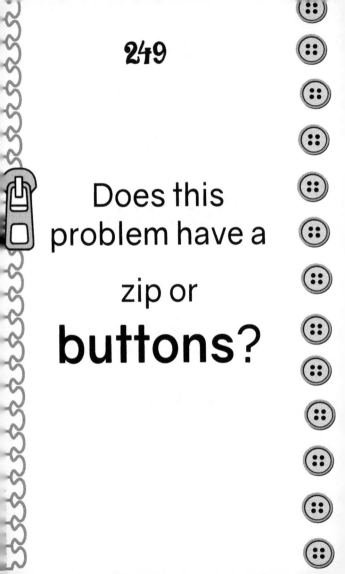

249

Does this problem have a

zip or

buttons?

250

What makes you so **lucky** that you could have a problem like this?

251

What kind of tree would make the problem?

252
Is the problem
sunrise or
sunset?

253

If you
painted the
problem
black,
who would
mistake it for
a part worn
car tyre?

254

If this problem were a piece of music, what music would it be?

255

How close do you have to get to the problem before you can't see it any more?

256

How does this problem secretly benefit you?

257

Is the problem in or out?

258

What is the problem's best side?

259

What would be our secret code word for this problem?

260

How small is the problem?

261

What does this problem symbolise?

262

What happens if you turn the contrast of the problem down?

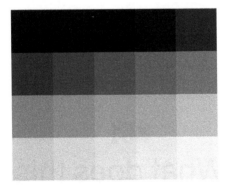

How would you

the problem?

264

Have you tried turning the problem off and

back on again?

265

How does the problem look through a looking glass?

266

Think of someone you know who you trust. What would they do?

267
Imagine it's a year from now. How has the problem changed?

268
What Confucius say about problem?

269

When you're a ghost, will you come back to haunt this problem?

Woooooohh

270

If you found this problem lost in the street, would you take it to a vet?

271

As you see yourself with that problem, what is interesting?

272
What gives you the right to have this problem?

273
HoW cUte iS the PRoBLeM?

274

What does this problem show?

275

Who can you depend on?

276

If this problem was a country, what would its

national

anthem

sound like?

277

WHEN YOU THROW
THE PROBLEM OUT
OF A WINDOW,
DOES IT BOUNCE OR
SPLATTER?

278

What is at the
end of the
problem?

279

Does the problem spiral to the left or right?

280

What kind of batteries does your problem take?

281

If you relax in a hot bath, how does the problem feel?

282
What would a steam roller do to the problem?

The Unsticker

283
Is the problem hot or cold?

284

What would happen if you got to work and realised you'd forgotten to take the problem with you?

285

Which well known song could be about the problem?

286

What wouldn't happen if you didn't?

287

What's the last thing you remember before the problem?

288

What types of flowers are connected to the problem?

289

Think of someone you know who you distrust. What would they do?

290

WHO COULD MAKE USE OF THIS PROBLEM?

291

If you made your problem quieter, would you still be able to see it?

292

What would the movie trailer for this problem be like?

293

How does the problem sound backwards?

294

In years to come, how will you be glad that you had this problem?

295

What would you be doing now if things were different?

296

At what temperature would your problem evaporate?

297

Does the problem go down the plughole clockwise or anticlockwise?

298

How much do you need this problem?

299

Can you think of a better question than this?

300

Are we talking about this problem or that problem?

As you get to the end of this question, what do you notice about that problem?

If this problem
was a bug,
would you
squash it or put it
 outside?

If you painted
the problem
yellow, would
anyone mistake
it for a big,
ripe, juicy,
tangy lemon?

304
Why isn't this problem rounder?

305
Is the problem high or low?

306

Is the problem high tide or low tide?

307
Was this a problem ten years ago?

308
If you painted the problem white, would anyone mistake it for a fluffy cloud?

309

As you see yourself with this problem, what do you notice first?

310

What wouldn't you do?

311

Would the problem make a nice ice sculpture?

312

Is the problem carbon neutral?

313

As you look back on this, which question was the hardest to answer?

314

How *fast* is the problem?

315

How would a bank robber break into the problem?

316

Is the problem light, dark or heavy?

317

Which part of this problem is the most furry?

318

If this problem were a car, what car would it be?

319

Should this problem go on a hot wash or a cool wash?

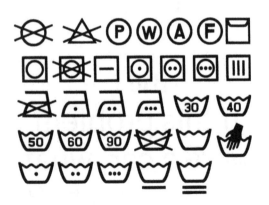

320
How would an owl hunt the problem?

321

Which TV
detective would
be able to solve
this problem?

322

How would a
child play with
the problem?

323

Is the problem **sausage** shaped or **donut** shaped?

324

Which way did

the problem

the problem

go?

325

As you drain the colour from the problem, which part can you see through first?

326

How long does the problem echo?

327

How many traffic cones would be needed to give the problem a contra-flow?

328

If the problem had a "do not touch" sign on it, would you?

329

Can you reach the problem from your favourite chair?

330

How long a bargepole would you need to poke the problem with?

331

Where are you going with this now?

332

WHICH REALITY TV SHOW WOULD THE PROBLEM WIN?

You've just opened the book at the back, haven't you? What would happen if you did the same with the problem?

Lightning Source UK Ltd.
Milton Keynes UK
UKHW020321240119
336107UK00005B/207